My Little Monster

Robico

CONTENTS

Yamaken
Shizuku Mizutani
Asako Natsume
Haru Yoshida
Sasayan
Takoyaki

STORY

When Shizuku Mizutani does a favor for problem child Haru Yoshida, who sat next to her in school, he develops a huge crush on her. Attracted to his innocence, she eventually falls for him, too. As the couple repeatedly fail to find themselves on the same page...they move on to their second year of high school. After that, Haru confesses his love, and the two finally become an official couple. Their courtship goes smoothly at first, but for some reason, Shizuku begins to feel jealous of Haru, and eventually she can no longer forgive the differences between him and herself. Then they have an argument at Haru's brother Yuzan's birthday party...and the next day, Haru stops going to school?!

CHAPTER 41: TWO WEEKS LATER

HUM
HUM
HUM...

HARU STOPPED COMING TO SCHOOL.
TWO WEEKS PASSED.
キンコーン
DING DONG

MIZUTANI-SAAAN!
MURMUR
ざわ
MURMUR
ざわ

HELLO, SHIMO-YANAGI-KUN.
CAN I HELP YOU?
MURMUR
WELL, I WAS HOPING YOU COULD ASK YOSHIDA-KUN TO GET AUTOGRAPHS FROM THE NASA ASTRONAUTS FOR ME.
KYA HA HA HA...
I REALLY LIKE UFOS AND STUFF.
MURMUR
?
...WAIT A SECOND. HARU'S AT NASA RIGHT NOW?
WHAT, HE'S NOT? THAT'S THE RUMOR I HEARD.
NO, I HEARD HE GOT IN A STREET FIGHT WITH THE COMMERCIAL HIGH SCHOOL'S FOUR HEAVENLY KINGS AND NOW HE'S IN THE HOSPITAL.
THAT'S YOSHIDA-KUN FOR YOU.
I THOUGHT HE WENT TO THE SAND DUNES IN TOTTORI.
NO, NO. HE GOT KIDNAPPED BY SOME RESEARCH LAB.
...
SQUEE
SQUEE
OH, MIZUTANI-SAN. YOSHIDA-KUN'S BEEN FORGETTING TO WATER THE FLOWERS.

...YOU, YUZAN THIS PARTY.
YOU CAN ALL GO TO HELL.
SINCE THAT DAY...
...I'VE SEEN NEITHER HIDE NOR HAIR OF HARU.
...I'VE LEFT MY CELL PHONE ON ALL THIS TIME.
BUT HE NEVER CALLS.
MIZUTANI-SAAAN!
WE'RE FROM THE GO CLUB. YOSHIDA-KUN WAS GOING TO JOIN. DO YOU KNOW IF HE'S STILL PLANNING TO DO THAT?
...YOU'LL HAVE TO ASK HIM YOURSELF.
AT THIS POINT, EVERYONE IN SCHOOL JUST ASSUMES IT'S ANOTHER ONE OF THE WEIRD THINGS HE DOES.
HE'S BEEN GOING TO GO CLUB, TOO?

IS IT...
...REALLY ALL MY FAULT?

SAEKO-SENSEI TOLD ME THAT HE HASN'T MISSED ENOUGH DAYS FOR IT TO BE A PROBLEM YET.
SINCE YOSHIDA-KUN ACTUALLY DOES TAKE HIS RESPON-SIBILITIES PRETTY SERIOUSLY.

I TALKED TO MITCHAN, AND HE SAYS YOSHIDA HASN'T BEEN HOME, EITHER.
WHAT CAN HE POSSIBLY BE DOING?

ALL MITTY WILL TELL US IS THAT THEY KIND OF HAD AN ARGUMENT.
NNNGH... AND HARU-KUN STILL WON'T ANSWER HIS PHONE.

DO YOU THINK MAYBE THEY BROKE UP?
H—
HOW CAN YOU SAY SUCH A THING, SASAYAN-KUN?!!
WHAT...?
HA HA HA
WELL, IF YOU LOOK AT IT THAT WAY, EVERYTHING MAKES SENSE.
IF YOSHIDA BROKE UP WITH MIZUTANI-SAN,
MAYBE HE DOESN'T SEE A POINT IN COMING TO SCHOOL ANYMORE.

NO!
...WHAT ARE YOU ALL DOING OUT HERE?

MITTY!
LET'S GO SEARCH FOR HARU-KUN TODAY! LOOK, I MADE A FLIER!
AND HOW WOULD THAT HELP?
SORRY, BUT THEY'RE POSTING THE TRIAL EXAM RESULTS TODAY.
AREN'T YOU WORRIED ABOUT HARU-KUN?!
...

I HATE YOU, MITTY!
STUPID DUMMY HEAD!
SIBERIAN TUNDRA FAIRY!
LOST
...NATSUME-SAN.
I THINK MIZUTANI-SAN IS WORRIED ABOUT YOSHIDA-KUN.
WHEN I TALKED TO SAEKO-SENSEI, SHE SAID THAT SHE HAD JUST BEEN IN TO ASK ABOUT HIM.
OSHIMA-SAN...
OH, IYO'S SEMPAIS.
YOU'RE ALL TOGETHER TODAY. HOW DO YOU DO?
IYO-CHAN.

GREETED SHIZUKU-SEMPAI WITH HER USUAL, "IF THINGS AREN'T WORKING OUT WITH YOU AND HARU-SEMPAI, THEN PLEASE LET IYO HAVE HIM," AND SHE DIDN'T REACT IN HER USUAL WAY.
IS SOMETHING THE MATTER?
THERE SHE GOES AGAIN. IT'S NOT FUNNY WHEN SHE SAYS IT.
...IT'S NOT A GOOD TIME TO JOKE LIKE THAT, IYO-CHAN.
I THINK MIZUTANI-SAN IS WORRIED.
SHE HASN'T HEARD FROM YOSHIDA-KUN IN A WHILE.
!
...
MY, MY.
WHAT GOOD WILL EVER COME OF A WOMAN FAWNING OVER ANOTHER WOMAN, OSHIMA-SEMPAI?
IYO BELIEVES THAT WOMEN LICKING EACH OTHER'S WOUNDS...
...IS NOTHING MORE THAN LUDICROUS.
...OH, DO YOU?
I DISAGREE.
RUMBLE RUMBLE

YOU ARE SO BLAND, OSHIMA-SEMPAI. DON'T THINK...
...JUST BECAUSE YOU HAVE A FOLLOWING AMONG SOME OF THE BOYS MEANS...
RAR RAR
...
IYO-CHAN, YOU'RE OUT! OUT!!
FWEEEET
YOU TWO! STOP THAT USELESS ARGUMENT RIGHT THIS INSTANT!
HA HA HA, WHOA, YAMAGUCHI-SAN.
YOU ACTUALLY MADE OSHIMA-SAN MAD.
...AND YOU, SASAYAN-KUN.
YOU'RE ACTING WEIRD, TOO.
HUH?

EVER SINCE THE SCHOOL FESTIVAL.
YOU HAVEN'T BEEN YOUR USUAL HAPPY SELF.

...WHAT? NO WAY.
I'M FINE.
OR SO YOU SAY, BUT YOU HAVE FEELINGS FOR HARU-SEMPAI, DON'T YOU?!
WHA-?!
OH.
WELL, OKAY THEN.
MISAWA BATTING CENTER NOW ACCEPTING MEMBERSHIPS!
PLAY THE NEWEST ARCADE GAMES!
I'M SORRY, SHIZUKU-CHAN.
I STILL HAVEN'T HEARD ANYTHING FROM THE LITTLE TWERP.
POINT CARDS

...I SEE.
MAN, THAT KID.
WHERE THE HELL IS HE?

HE CALLS ME OUT OF THE BLUE.
OW! OW!! WHAT THE HELL ARE YOU DOING?!
KAPOW KAPOW POW
OH, MITCHAN? SORRY, BUT I'M NOT GONNA BE HOME FOR A WHILE.
...AND THAT WAS THE LAST I EVER HEARD OF HIM.
A PRETTY SPIRITED DISAPPEAR-ANCE.

WELL, I DOUBT...
...HE WOULD DO ANYTHING TO REALLY WORRY YOU.

UM.
WHERE'S YUZAN-SAN?
YUZAN? HE SAYS HE'S BUSY WITH COLLEGE RIGHT NOW. I DON'T THINK HE'LL BE COMING BY FOR A WHILE.
IS SOME-THING WRONG?
...NO.
WELL, THANK YOU FOR YOUR TIME.

HEY, SHIZUKU-CHAN.
IF HARU CALLS, I'LL TELL HIM TO CALL YOU, OKAY?

IT REALLY IS...
...MY FAULT, ISN'T IT?

THAT'S THE ONLY THING I CAN THINK OF.
I MEAN, THAT DAY,
THERE WAS A LOOK ON HARU'S FACE THAT I'D NEVER SEEN BEFORE.

AND I
CAN'T EVEN
APOLOGIZE.
THAT'S
NOT FAIR.

...
SIGH...
IYO...
...WENT TO A COED SCHOOL SO SHE COULD FIND A HANDSOME MAN AND A BEAUTIFUL ROMANCE.
SO WHY MUST SHE HAVE TEA WITH THESE LOWLIFES?!

IYO WANTS A BOYFRIEND, TOO! IYO WANTS A BOYFRIEND, TOO!!
GOT AN ANTI-DOTE?
HOLD ON A SEC.
...HEY.
YAMAKEN.
DO SOMETHING ABOUT YOUR DNA. SHE'S GETTING ON MY NERVES.
SORRY TO BREAK IT TO YOU, BUT SHE'S ADOPTED.
MY DEAR BROTHER?!
CLANG
IYO, YOU'RE A PAIN IN THE ASS. GO GET YOUR BELOVED HARU-SEMPAI TO BANG YOU.
MUST YOU BE SO VULGAR?!
OH, DON'T BE SILLY.
I MEAN, IYO WANTS TO SEE HIM.
THIS IS IYO'S CHANCE. SHE WOULD LOVE NOTHING MORE THAN TO GO SEE HARU-SEMPAI, BUT HE'S NOT COMING TO SCHOOL.
WHEN DID YOU EVER HAVE A CHANCE?
KEEP YOUR DREAMS IN DREAMLAND. I'LL TREAT YOU RIGHT IN THE END.
HE'S BEEN GONE FOR TWO WHOLE WEEKS AND HASN'T EVEN INFORMED HIS GIRLFRIEND OF HIS WHERE-ABOUTS. OBVIOUSLY SOMETHING HAPPENED BETWEEN THEM.
IYO IS TOLD THAT EVEN SHIZUKU-SEMPAI HASN'T BEEN ABLE TO REACH HIM.

WHOA, REALLY?
I JUST SAW 'EM BOTH AT HIS FAMILY'S PARTY, AND THEY WERE ACTING TOTALLY NORMAL.
IYO WISHES SHE COULD HAVE GONE!
THEN SOMETHING MUST HAVE HAPPENED AFTER THAT.
HOW CAN YOU BE SO SURE?

WHATEVER HAPPENED, SHIZUKU-SEMPAI HASN'T BEEN HERSELF.
IT'S NO FUN FOR IYO!
CLATTER
...LATER.
I'M OFF TO CRAM SCHOOL.

BEEP
Guess who this is!
...UGH.
WHAT IS HE DOING?

WELL.
IT'S NOT MY PROBLEM.

CRUNCH
TEA

CRUNCH
SEN BEI
TEA
MUNCH MUNCH
MUNCH
...
SNAP
CRUNCH CRUNCH
HEY!
CRUNCH
SEN

LADIES...
...DO NOT LIE AROUND THE STREET EATING RICE CRACKERS.
...
YAMAKEN-KUN.
YOU DIDN'T DO SO HOT ON THIS LAST TRIAL EXAM, DID YOU?
YOU LITTLE...
CRUNCH
TEA
SEN BEI

SO I HEARD...
...HARU DITCHED YOU?
IS THAT WHY YOU'RE OUT HERE WALLOWING?
WHAT A CHEAP WOMAN.
...THAT'S NONE OF YOUR BUSINESS, YAMAKEN-KUN.
CRUNCH
TCH.
I...
...HAVE FEELINGS, TOO.
I DIDN'T THINK IT WOULD TURN INTO SUCH A BIG DEAL.
FOR ONE THING,
I DIDN'T DO ANY-THING HE COULD PRESS CHARGES FOR.
IS...
IS SHE...
AND HE...
...JUST UP AND...
WHAT-EVER.
IF THAT'S HOW HE FEELS, THEN I'M TOO STRESSED OUT TO TALK ABOUT IT ANYWAY.
...REALLY THAT BITTER?!
MUNCH MUNCH

I WAS REJECTED...
...BY THIS?!!
ZSHHH
I CAN'T EVEN GUESS WHAT HAPPENED.
YOU'VE NEVER...
...MADE SOMEONE HATE YOU BEFORE, HAVE YOU?
SEN BEI
YOU'VE NEVER REALLY THOUGHT ABOUT HOW THE THINGS YOU SAY WOULD AFFECT SOME-ONE,
OR HAD WORDS STICK IN YOUR THROAT, BECAUSE YOU WERE AFRAID SOMEONE WOULD STOP LIKING YOU, HAVE YOU?
HEH.
SERVES YOU RIGHT.

...ARE YOU SAYING IT'S MY FAULT THEN?
I DON'T KNOW, MAYBE.
I DON'T KNOW WHAT'S GOING ON BETWEEN YOU GUYS.
TMP
BUT ANYWAY,

IF YOU'RE HAVING TROUBLE,
I WOULDN'T MIND IF YOU WANT TO TALK TO ME ABOUT IT.

THANKS,
BUT I'M FINE.
I JUST GOT MY THOUGHTS IN ORDER.
YOU'RE RIGHT. TURNING IT OVER IN MY OWN HEAD ISN'T GOING TO HELP ANYTHING.
I HAVE TO SEE HARU.
THIS IS ABOUT BOTH OF US.

OH. OKAY.
IT'S BEEN A WHILE, HASN'T IT, YAMAKEN-KUN?
IF YOU LIKE, I CAN WALK YOU TO THE BUS STOP.
PAT PAT
ぱん
ぱん
I DON'T NEED HELP.
BUT YOU WERE JUST WALKING IN CIRCLES UNTIL YOU STOPPED AND TALKED TO ME.
F YOU SAW E, YOU HOULD HAVE AID HI.
?
YOU SAID YOU DIDN'T WANT TO BE FRIENDS.
...BUT YAMAKEN-KUN.
I THOUGHT YOU DUMPED ME.
WHA?!
WHEN DID I—?
...
...

DECIDED TO HAVE HER GUIDE HIM AFTER ALL.

"WELL, DO YOU UNDERSTAND HOW I FEEL?"
"YOU DON'T UNDERSTAND HOW I FEEL."
WHEN HE SAID THAT,
IT WAS THE FIRST TIME I REALIZED...
...HOW USELESS IT IS TO BE LIKE THAT.
YAMAKEN-KUN,
I REALIZED SOMETHING AT HARU'S FAMILY'S PARTY.
IF I WANT TO BE UNDERSTOOD,
I NEED TO PUT IN THE EFFORT.

I REALIZED WHY...
...I'M SO OBSESSED WITH STUDYING.
I WAS TRYING NOT TO NOTICE,
TRYING NOT TO GET HURT.
I WAS AFRAID...
...THAT MAYBE I WASN'T...
...NEEDED.
...WELL, IN A NUTSHELL, I HAD ALWAYS THOUGHT THAT HARU AND I WERE BIRDS OF A FEATHER, AND THEN IT TURNED OUT WE WEREN'T, SO I GOT MAD AT HIM WHEN HE HAD EVERY RIGHT TO BE MAD AT ME.
YOU'RE A TERRIBLE PERSON.

...YEA
I THINK SO, TOO.
IT'S ONLY FAIR FOR HARU TO BE UPSET.
I...
...WAS ANNOYED.
AND I TOOK IT OUT ON HIM.
...IT'S OKAY...
FOR YOU TO BE LIKE THAT.
YOU'RE HONEST TO A FAULT.
IT'S OKAY FOR YOU TO MAKE HIM FACE THAT.

ISN'T THAT WHY...
...HARU...
...FELL FOR YOU IN THE FIRST PLACE?

...OH, OKAY.
I WISH
I HAD LISTENED TO HARU MORE.
I WISH...
...I HAD LOOKED UP AT HIM.

ALL THIS TIME,
HARU'S BEEN WANTING A CONNECTION.
I FEEL LIKE ONE DAY,
YOU'LL JUST WRITE ME OFF WITH AN "OH WELL," TOO.
GIVE ME A BREAK.
IF I COULD DO THAT, NONE OF THIS WOULD HAVE HAPPENED.
YOU THINK I'M GOING TO LET IT END LIKE THIS?

"DID YOU GE SCARED THAT YOU GET HUR AGAIN?"

WELL?
DO YOU HAVE ANY IDEA WHERE HARU IS NOW?
OH.
I WAS JUST THINKING ABOUT THAT.
Flower

RIGHT NOW, MY BEST GUESS IS HE'S ON A TUNA BOAT.
IF HE IS, I'LL HAVE TO BE READY FOR A LONG STRUGGLE.
I ACTUALLY WANT TO KNOW HOW IN THE WORLD YOU CAME UP WITH THAT.

...HM?

...HUH? WAIT.
A PART OF ME WAS ALWAYS SURE THAT HARU WAS JUST GOING TO COME BACK LIKE HE ALWAYS DOES.
BUT IF, FOR HE SAKE OF RGUMENT, HE ID RUN OFF SOMEWHERE ECAUSE OF OUR FIGHT...

...IS IT POSSIBLE THAT HE'LL STAY AWAY FOREVER?!
CLANG...
ガーッ…
JUST REALIZED.
?

CLANG CLANG
BEEP BEEP
...
A TUNA BOAT, EH?
TELLLL...
OH.
IT'S ACTUALLY RINGING.
TELLLLL
TELLLL...
BEEP
WHAT?
HEY.
WHAT ARE YOU DOING, STUPID?
AH?
WHAT AM *I* DOING?

TAKOYAKI
12 PIECE
TAKOYAKI
6 PIECE
WITH LOTS OCTOPUS.
TAKOYAKI

WITH LOTS OCTOPUS!
TAKOYAKI

...
TAKOYAKI 6 PIECE
TAKOYAKI 12 PIECE

WHAT ARE YOU DOING, HARU?
...

EAT...
EATING TAKOYAKI?

I CAN SEE THAT!!
HE WAS CLOSER THAN I REALIZED.

TWO WEEKS LATER

WHAT? YOSHIDA-KUN STILL HASN'T COME TO SCHOOL?
ざわ MURMUR
I BROUGHT COOKIES TO THANK HIM FOR PLAYING SHOGI.
MURMUR ざわ

THE VIOLAS ARE BLOOMING. YOSHIDA REALLY WANTED TO SEE THAT. MAYBE I SHOULD TEXT HIM A PICTURE.
UM...IS YOSHIDA-SEMPAI HERE?

ワイ WALLA
I BROUGHT HIM THE NEXT VOLUME IN THAT MANGA HE WAS BORROWING.
THAT TABLE TENNIS MATCH...
I FOUND A GOOD HAIR STRAIGHTENER.
WALLA ワイ

WHERE DID ALL THESE FRIENDS COME FROM?
SO MY DOG HAD PUPPIES, AND...
UPON LEAVING THE CLASSROOM, A NEW FACT COMES TO LIGHT.

A GIFT FROM MA-BO

ピ BEEP...
Guess who this is!

ピ BEEP
She's a different person!
ピ BEEP

ピ BEEP...

...WELL.
IT'S NOT MY PROBLEM.
AFTER TAKING A GOOD LOOK AT ALL OF THEM, HE CLOSED THE CONVERSATION.

ON THE DAY OF YUZAN-SAN'S PARTY
DING-ALING
!?

CHAPTER 42:
MERRY-GO-ROUND
NNNGH...
SMACK...
LOST
IF YOU RECOGNIZE THIS FACE CALL THIS NUMBER
ASAKO NATSUME 090-XXXX-0000
golbeza@...
WARNING: IF YOU APPROACH HIM WITHOUT WARNING, YOU MAY GET HURT. IF YOU SEE HIM; DO NOT SPEAK TO HIM. CALL THE NUMBER!
STAY
ALIVE
I WONDER WHERE HARU-KUN IS, AND WHAT HE'S DOING NOW...

I HOPE HE'S NOT STARVING AND ALONE SOMEWHERE.
I HOPE HE'S NOT HURT AND UNABLE TO MOVE...
NATSUME-CHAN, POSTING THAT HERE ISN'T GOING TO HELP ANYTHING.
IS HE A LOST DOG?
SHOYO

...WHY ARE YOU SO WORRIED ABOUT HIM, NATSUME-SAN?
I MEAN, I AM, TOO, BUT...

AT TIMES LIKE THIS, GIRLS ARE SUPPOSED TO MAKE A BIG DEAL ABOUT THEIR FRIENDS' CRISES.
THEY GET TOGETHER TO TRY TO COME UP WITH A SOLUTION.
THEY THINK AS HARD AS THEY CAN.
...NOT THAT I'VE EVER BEEN INCLUDED IN THAT KIND OF THING BEFORE.
SINCE I WAS USUALLY THE CAUSE OF THE FRIEND'S CRISIS...
WAAAH! MA-KUN SAYS HE LIKES NATSUME!
LOST
UH-HUH...

IT'S MITTY.
SHE'S PRETEN-DING SHE DOESN'T CARE.

"I SHOULD NEVER
HAVE MADE FRIENDS WITH HER."
IF THERE'S ANYTHING YOU CAN DO,
WOULDN'T YOU WANT TO DO IT?
AND MAYBE MITTY WON'T TELL ME ANY-THING.
BUT WE'RE FRIENDS.
...AND HARU-KUN ISN'T HELPING!
IF HE HAS A PROBLEM, WOULD IT KILL HIM TO SAY *SOMETHING* ABOUT IT?
WHAT DO THEY TAKE ME FOR?!
AAAH! NOW THAT I'M THINKING ABOUT IT, THE TEARS ARE BACK.
グチ GRUMBLE
グチ GRUMBLE
...IT'S OKAY, NATSUME-SAN.
GIVE 'EM TIME, THEY'LL—
HA HA HA!

HA HA HA...
HEY, THOSE ARE...
...THE KIDS FROM MY JUNIOR HIGH WHO GO TO COMMERCE SCHOOL NOW.
...
I'M SORRY. I GUESS I STARTED WHINING.
HEH HEH HEH.
OKAY!! THE FLIERS ARE UP, SO LET'S GO SEE ABOUT THOSE MELON BUNS I'VE HAD MY EYE ON.
SORRY, I RAN INTO SOME FRIENDS.
I HATE TO DO THIS, NATSUME-SAN, BUT COULD YOU GO ON WITHOUT ME?!

WHAT?! THEN WHAT ARE WE GONNA DO ABOUT THE LIMITED EDITION MELON BUNS?! THEY'LL ONLY SELL ONE PER CUSTOMER!
I'M REALLY SORRY!
I HAVE TO PASS TODAY!
...
MELON BUNS
LIMITED TIME
EAT AND-

BUT YOU SAID
YOU WANTED ONE!!

HE'S ALWAYS, ALWAYS GOING OFF ABOUT HIS FRIENDS!
SO WHAT AM I THEN?!
IS HANGING OUT WITH "THE GUYS" THAT GREAT?!!
FUME
FUME
FOR SOMEONE WHO SUPPOSEDLY LIKES ME,
HE'S NOT ACTING LIKE IT AT ALL!
YO, LONG TIME NO SEE!
HEY, SASAYAN!
SLIGHTED
WELL THAT'S JUST FINE! I'M THE ONE WHO TOLD HIM TO FORGET ABOUT IT!!
HMPH! I DON'T NEED SASAYAN-KUN!
HMP
WHEN HARU-KUN COMES BACK, I CAN GO GET MELON BUNS WITH HIM!
...
HARU-KUN.
SNIFFLE
I HOPE HE COMES BACK SOON.
WITH LOTS OF OCTOPUS!
TAKOYAKI

HEY.
I JUST GOT THROUGH TO HARU FOR A SEC...
...
TAKOYAKI
...
MAKEN-KUN.

GLOMP
HEY THERE, HARU.
WHERE *HAVE* YOU BEEN ALL THIS TIME?
OF COURSE, WITH YOU GONE, *WE'VE* BEEN HAVING A GREAT TIME.
?!
Y-YAMAKEN KUN?! YOU WEREN'T ACTING REMOTELY LIKE THIS A MINUTE AGO...
GASP
D-DON'T TELL ME, YOU WERE ONLY BEING FRIENDLY TO TRICK ME?!
...WOULD YOU BE QUIET FOR A SECOND?
TAKOYAKI
OH.
SEE YA.
TAKOYA

...THAT WAS TOO EASY.
DID HE ACTUALLY GIVE UP ON YOU?
...
PAH
...SORRY ABOUT THAT.
I JUST HAD TO CHECK.
THAT'S OKAY...
ALL THIS TIME,
NOW I KNOW FOR SURE.
A PART OF ME THOUGHT HE WAS JUST OFF ON...
...AN-OTHER ONE OF HIS WHIMS.

SO HARU REALLY...
...WAS AVOIDING ME.
...HEY.
ARE YOU IN SHOCK? OR IS THIS SOME KIND OF GAG?
YOU'RE CLEARLY UPSET.
...AND AS USUAL.
I'M NOT EVEN A BLIP ON YOUR RADAR, AM I?
WELL, WHATEVER.

CLANG
CLANG
CLANG
CLANG
カンカンカンカン

...

FOR REAL?
SLUMP
CLANG
CLANG
CLANG
CLANG
カンカンカンカン

IT'S ONLY BEEN TWO WEEKS.
SUPER FUN!
AND I...
HOW DID THAT HAPPEN?!
I...

ALL I COULD DO WAS SIT THERE AND EAT TAKO-YAKI!!
WHOA!

WHAT ARE YOU DOING OUT HERE, YOSHIDA?
AND HEY, WHERE HAVE YOU BEEN?
SASAYAN...
I RAN INTO A GUY MY AUNT KNEW
ON THE WAY HOME FROM YUZAN'S BIRTHDAY PARTY.
HEY, HARU-KUN.
GOING HOME? IF YOU LIKE, WHY NOT COME VISIT ME?
OCEANIC
A RESEARCH LAB?!

AHH?
BAM!
WHO'D WANNA VISIT YOU?!
SKFF SKFF SKFF SKFF
RATTLE
YOU'RE SO ANNOYING!
KIRIYA-SENSEI SAID GET IN— NOW GET IN!
KAPOW!
DAMMIT, THAT HURT!
WHAT ARE YOU DO—
HA HA HA. GOTODA-SAN CAN BE A LITTLE EXTREME.
NOW LET'S GET OUT OF HERE.
BAM!
...SO I ENDED UP STAYING WITH THAT KIRIYA GUY.
THAT'S KIDNAP-PING, ISN'T IT?
NAH, I COULD'VE ESCAPED IF I WANTED TO.
I JUST DIDN'T REALLY CARE ANY-MORE.
SO I SPENT MY TIME HELPING KIRIYA.
AND THAT WAS RETTY FUN.

HAWAI'I
BUT THEN IT HIT ME.
I REALLY...
MISS SHIZUKU.
...AND NOW I JUST GOT BACK.
BUT THEN I RAN INTO SHIZUKU AND YAMAKEN, AND MY FACE IS POSTED ALL OVER TOWN.
I DON'T KNOW WHAT'S WHAT ANYMORE...
OH, THAT WAS NATSUME-SAN'S DOING.
THEY'VE BEEN WORRIED ABOUT YOU.
NATSUME-SAN AND MIZUTANI-SAN BOTH.

I DON'T THINK...
...I'M THE KIND OF GUY WHO CAN UNDERSTAND THE SUBTLETIES OF THE HUMAN HEART.
HACK!

...WHAT'S WRONG, SASAYAN?

IT'S JUST, YOU SAID THAT WITH SUCH A STRAIGHT FACE...
I MEAN...
...IS THAT WHAT YOU'VE BEEN THINKING ABOUT?!

THE LAST TIME I SAW SHIZUKU, I SAID SOME MEAN THINGS TO HER. I WANTED TO APOLOGIZE.
BUT I DON'T EVEN KNOW WHAT STARTED IT.
SO THAT'S THE CONCLUSION I CAME TO.
...

I DON'T KNOW WHAT HAPPENED, BUT I'M PRETTY SURE IT WASN'T JUST ONE OF YOU WHO STARTED IT.
I MEAN, YOSHIDA.
YOU'RE PRETTY STUPID.

...GOT A PROBLEM WITH THAT?
DAMMIT, YOU'RE LUCKY, SASAYAN.
YOU NEVER HAVE TO WORRY ABOUT STUFF LIKE THIS.
WHAT? I WORRY ABOUT STUFF.
WELL, I GUESS I'M NOT *WORRIED*
SO MUCH AS UNSURE.
CLACK
REMEMBER WHEN I TOLD YOU THERE WAS THIS JERK ON MY JUNIOR HIGH BASEBALL TEAM?
YOU MEAN THE GUY YOU HATED THAT I HELPED AND YOU DIDN'T?
GOOD MEMORY.
YEAH. HIS NAME'S SHINJO.
I HAPPENED TO RUN INTO HIM AT THE SCHOOL FESTIVAL.

HE'S GOING TO A COMMERCE SCHOOL THESE DAYS.
HE QUIT BASE-BALL.
SO GO. WHAT'S THE PROBLEM?
IF HE WANTS YOU TO.
YOU MAKE IT SOUND SO SIMPLE. ᵕ
AND NOW HE'S DOING SOMETHING ELSE. HE WANTS ME TO GO SEE HIM.
HE EVEN GAVE ME TICKETS.
THE GUYS IN MY YEAR WERE SUSPENDED FROM THE TEAM BECAUSE OF HIM.
AND A LOT'S HAPPENED.

IT'S NOT LIKE I CAN FORGET ALL THAT...
...JUST BECAUSE HE COMES ALONG AND ACTS LIKE NOTHING HAPPENED.

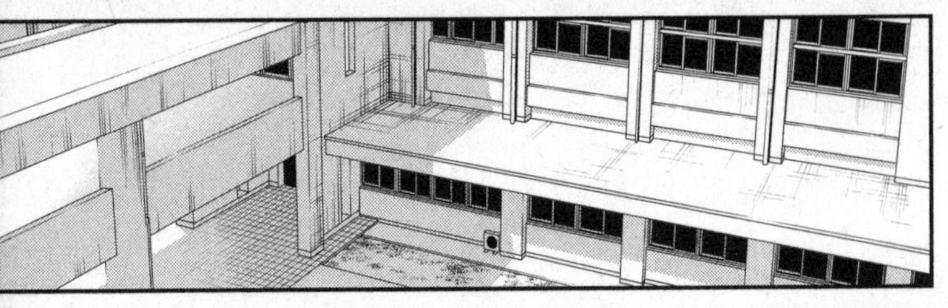

I SAID I DON'T FEE THAT WAY ANYMORE.
DO YOU HAVE TO BE IN LOVE WITH SOMEONE TO BE WORRIED ABOUT THEM?

ANY-MORE?
SO YOU *DID* LIKE HIM, OSHIMA-SEMPAI.
YOU SHOULD JUST BE HONEST WITH EVERYONE AND SAY, "I'M AFTER YOSHIDA-KUN."

WHA-!
UGH, GIRLS! WE ARE IN THE MIDDLE OF A LUNCH MEETING!!
YOU ONLY DROPPED OUT OF THE RACE OUT OF CONSIDERATION FOR SHIZUKU-SEMPAI, DIDN'T YOU?
WE'RE PLANNING OPERATION: FIND HARU-KUN!
VVVN VVVN
HELLO...? YES... YES... I AM IN HIGH SCHOOL.
NO... I AM NOT LOOKING FOR ANYTHING OF THE SORT.
WELL? WELL? HAVE YOU CONFESSED TO HIM?
DARNIT... I SHOULDN'T HAVE PUT MY NUMBER ON THE FLIER.
I'M GETTING SO MANY WEIRD CALLS.
WHAT? SHINJO?
HE DOESN'T PLAY BASEBALL ANYMORE.
...WHY DID HE QUIT?
HE WAS THE BEST PLAYER ON THE TEAM.

ARE YOU STILL HANGING OUT WITH THOSE GUYS?
YOU GUYS DISGUST ME.
SERIOUSLY.
...WHAT AR THESE?
WHY ARE YOU GIVING THEM TO ME?
HUH? BECAUSE.
YOU'RE THE ONLY ONE ON THE TEAM WHO WOULD TALK TO ME.
HATED YOUR GUTS.
IF I HAD
STOOD UP FOR HIM THROUGH IT ALL,
MAYBE SHINJO WOULDN'T HAVE QUIT BASEBALL.
BUT...
I'M PROBABLY OVER-THINKING IT.
...WHAT IS MR. POPULAR SASAYAN-KUN
DOING IN A PLACE LIKE THIS?

TSUME-SAN.
...
NOT THAT AGAIN.
IF YOU'RE MAD ABOUT YESTERDAY, I'M SORRY.
NOW LEAVE ME ALONE.
UGH, I'M HOPELESS.
...I'M BUMMED OUT RIGHT NOW.
I DON'T WANT YOU TO SEE ME.
WHY CAN I ONLY SAY THINGS THAT WILL MAKE HER MAD?

YEAH.
WELL.
THAT'S HOW IT IS...
WHEN YOU'RE DEPRESSED.
HUH?
YOU'RE NOT BEING FAIR, SASAYAN-KUN.
YOU'RE *ALWAYS* SURROUNDED BY PEOPLE.
BUT NOW THAT YOU'RE DEPRESSED, YOU'RE ALL ALONE.

...I FEEL BAD LEAVING PEOPLE ALONE.
SO I'LL STAY HERE WITH YOU.

PFFT!
...WHAT'S THAT MEAN?
LIKE YOU'RE SO IMPORTANT!
H—
HEH HEH HEH.
HEY, WHEN IT COMES TO BEING DEPRESSED, I'M A PRO!
IF YOU'RE ALONE AT A TIME LIKE THIS...
...YOUR THOUGHTS KEEP GOING FROM BAD TO WORSE.
?!

WHA–
WHA–
...YEAH.
THEY REALLY DO.
...SORRY.
WILL YOU LET ME STAY LIKE THIS...
...
...JUST FOR A MINUTE?

S—
SO YOU KNOW,
I'M JUST DOING THIS TO REPAY YOU.
YEAH.
'CAUSE YOU'RE ALWAYS
DOING NICE THINGS FOR ME.
YEAH.

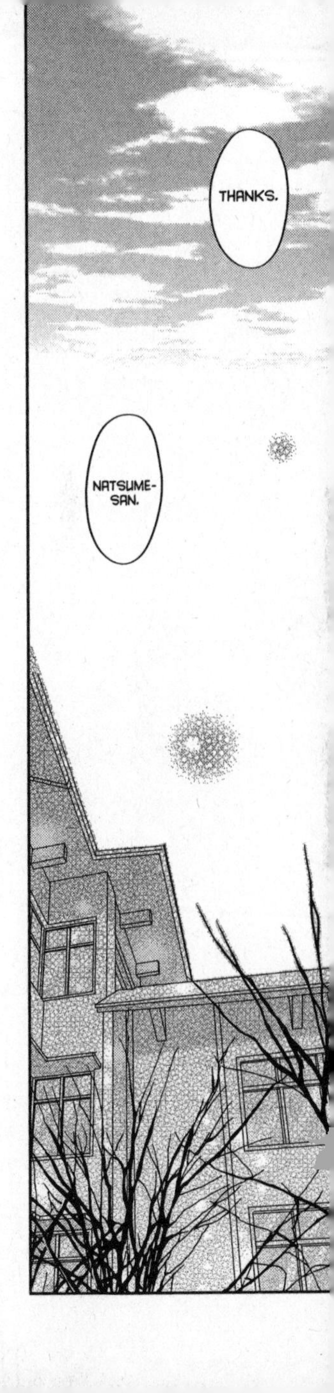
THANKS.
NATSUME-SAN.

LIBRARY

...

OH!! THERE YOU ARE, MITTY! I HAVE GOOD NEWS!!

SASAYAN-KUN SAYS HE RAN INTO HARU-KUN YESTERDAY!
OH.
I SAW HARU YESTERDAY, TOO.

OH! YOU DID, HUH?
THEN LET'S ALL GO AFTER SCHOOL TO—
...SORRY.
CLATTER
ガタ
BUT NO THANKS. I'LL PASS.

...WHAT'S WRONG, MITTY? DIDN'T YOU MAKE UP WITH HARU-KUN?
...

I DON'T THINK...
...HE NEEDS ME ANYMORE.

WHAT? DID HE TELL YOU THAT?
I'M SORRY, NATSUME-SAN.
SENSEI WANTED TO SEE ME.
MITTY!
WAIT, PLEASE!
MI...
I SAID WAIT!!
WHAM
KONK
THUD THUD THUD...
FSHHH

...
NATSUME-SAN. WHAT ARE YOU DOING?
FSHHH
BUT
LET'S GIVE YOU LIKE A MILLION BENEFITS OF THE DOUBT,
AND SAY HARU-KUN REALLY THINKS THAT.
THEN SO WHAT?
ARE YOU OKAY WITH THAT, MITTY?
WHY DO YOU ALWAYS
MAKE UP YOUR MIND
WITHOUT EVER TALKING TO ANYBODY ELSE?!!
WELL, I...
THE ONLY HARU I KNOW IS THE ONE WHO LIKES ME.

I HAVEN'T APOLOGIZE YET.
I WANT TO SIT DOWN AND TALK WITH HIM.
BUT NOW
I THINK HE HATES ME.
HARU
MIGHT NOT...
...EVER LISTEN TO ME AGAIN!!
IT'S OKAY,
MITTY.

EVEN IF HE IS MAD,
IF YOU ASK HARU-KUN TO LISTEN TO YOU,
I'M SURE HE WOULD.

OKAY?
AND HEY, AFTER YOU'VE BEEN REJECTED IS WHEN LIFE TRULY BEGINS!!
!!
DU-DUN
DON'T WORRY! I'LL BE THERE TO PICK UP YOUR REMAINS!
...
DING DONG...
H...THE BELL.

YOU WER SUPPOSE TO GO TO THE FACULTY ROOM.
YOU GO ON. I'LL CLEAN THIS UP.
SORRY.
...
NATSUME-SAN.
THANK YOU.
I'LL GIVE IT ANOTHER TRY.
I'M GLAD
YOU
AND HARU
AND I ARE FRIENDS.

キンコーン
DING DONG...
MURMUR
ザワ
ザワ
MURMUR
FWEEET
ピー
GET TOGETHER, EVERYONE!
MURMUR
ザワ
KYA HA HA HA
MURMUR...
ザワ...
I'M GLAD YOU AND HARU AND I...
...ARE FRIENDS.
...HNNH
NNH.

HNN-NNH!
SOB SOB
ポロ
ポロ
SOB...
ポロ...
SASAYAN.
SYOYO

YOSHI-DA?!
WHAT HAPPENED TO YOUR FACE?
MITCHAN BEAT ME UP.
TOLD ME NOT TO WORRY HIM.
SO HEY, SASAYAN.
I'VE BEEN THINKING SINCE LAST NIGHT.

IF YOU'RE SO UNSURE, I THINK YOU SHOULD JUST GO.
SEE THAT SHINJO GUY.

...
YOU CAME ALL THE WAY OUT HERE TO TELL ME THAT?
I WAS HERE TO CHECK ON NAGOYA ANYWAY.

...YEAH, I WAS JUST THINKING THE SAME THING!
TEP
WAIT A SECOND, YOSHIDA.
PRACTICE IS ALMOST OVER; I'LL WALK HOME WITH YOU!

SO WHAT ARE YOU DOING ABOUT SCHOOL, YOSHIDA?
HUH? I'LL START GOING TOMORROW.
I PROMISED OTOMO-KUN THAT I'D BE IN THE GO TOURNAMENT.
OH.
AND I WANT
TO TALK TO SHIZUKU.
SO I'M PLANNING TO AMBUSH HER ON THE WAY TO SCHOOL TOMORROW. WHAT DO YOU THINK?
...MAYBE A NORMAL APOLOGY WOULD BE BETTER.
ANYWAY, NATSUME-SAN'S BEEN SO WORRIED ABOUT YOU THAT SHE WON'T GIVE ME THE TIME OF DAY.
WHAT DO YOU THINK I SHOULD DO?
WHAT?!
ピロリン
DING-ALING
From NATSUME-SAN
Sub MITTY
Good news!
According to Sasayan-kun's report, Haru-kun is coming to school tomorrow

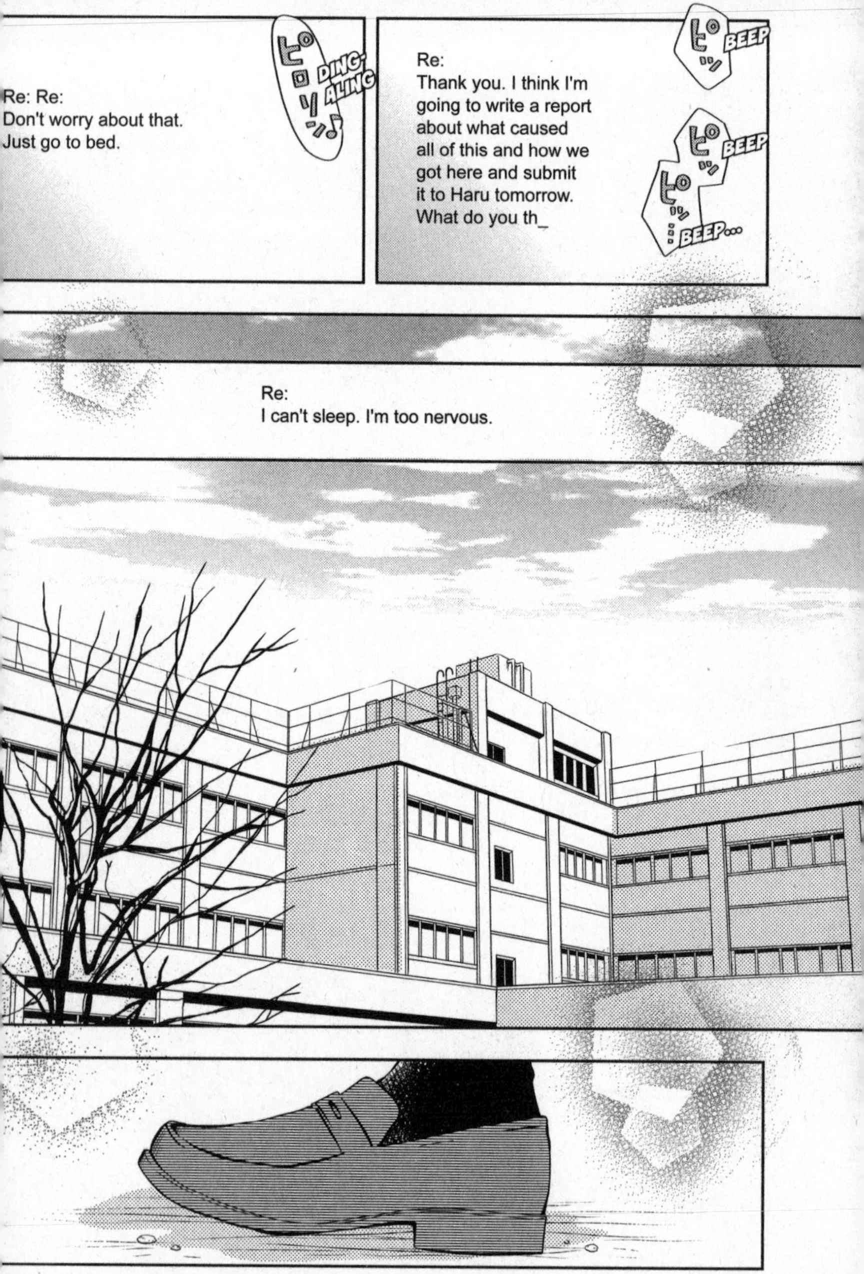

Re:
Thank you. I think I'm
going to write a report
about what caused
all of this and how we
got here and submit
it to Haru tomorrow.
What do you th_

BEEP

BEEP

BEEP...

DING-ALING

Re: Re:
Don't worry about that.
Just go to bed.

Re:
I can't sleep. I'm too nervous.

MURMUR
ザワ
MURMUR
ザワ

HARU-KUN...!!
SORRY I WAS GONE SO LONG, NATSUME.
TOUCHED...
HEY, IT'S YOSHIDA-KUN!
GOOD MORNING!

THAT'S OKAY! THAT'S OKAY!
BECAUSE I AM YOUR AND MITTY'S IRREPLACEABLE FRIEND.
YOU'RE NOT SUPPOSED TO CALL YOURSELF THAT.
HEY, YOSHIDA-KUN'S HERE!
HEH HEH...♡ LAST NIGHT WAS REALLY TOUGH! ♡

OH! THERE SHE IS! MITTY!!
B-DMP

HI!
GOOD MORNING!

ザワ
MURMUR
HEY, YOSHIDA-KUN!
HI THERE!
MURMUR
ザワ

MURMUR
ザワ
GOOD MORNING.
HELLO!
'MORNING.

...
スイッ WHIRL
!!

EXCUSE ME, MITTY!! THIS IS NOT THE STRATEGY YO MENTIONED LAST NIGHT!!
I-I KNOW! I KNOW, BUT!
...
LIKE A FROG BEING GLARED AT BY A SNAKE.
BOCK
キンコーンカーン
DING DONG...
ザワ
MURMUR
ザワ
MURMUR

ザワ
MURMUR
ザワ
MURMUR
SHOYO HIGH SCHOOL
ザワ
MURMUR

WALKING HOME

SO, SASAYAN. YOU LIKE NATSUME?
YOU BETTER NOT SAY ANYTHING WEIRD.
OKAY.

BUT, MAN. SHE DOESN'T TRUST GUYS. THAT'S GONNA BE HARD.
SHE THINKS "GUY WHO LIKES HER" EQUALS "GUY WHO DOESN'T GET IT."
...YOU REALLY UNDER-STAND HER, DON'T YOU?

WELL, SHE TALKS MORE THAN ANY-BODY.
...IF ONLY MIZUTANI-SAN DID.

BUT I'M KINDA RELIEVED. I WAS AFRAID IF I MADE A WRONG MOVE, I'D END UP SUPPORTING NATSUME THE REST OF MY LIFE.
LIKE TAKING IN AN ANIMAL.
...I DON'T KNOW. SHE'S REJECTING ME PRETTY HARD-CORE.

WHY? YOU KNOW HER PERSONALLY.
THAT'S WHY YOU LIKE HER, RIGHT?
...

...UH, OH YEAH, YOSHIDA. I'M GOING TO SEE SHINJO ON OUR NEXT DAY OFF. COME WITH ME.
I HAVE TWO TICKETS.
WHY DID YOU CHANGE THE SUBJECT?
I DIDN'T.

LATER, THEY WENT TO SEE SHINJO.
A CONCERT, HUH?
WHAT'S WITH THAT MAKE-UP?!!
IT WAS A DEATH METAL CONCERT.

CHAPTER 43:
TWO IN A DREAM

ONIWA
summer

LISTEN, NATSUME.

MEN ARE NOT THE ENEMY.

I'M NOT REALLY ONE TO SAY THIS.

BUT HUMANS ARE NOT THE ENEMY.

WHERE IS THIS COMING FROM?

HERE, YOSHIDA-KUN. I TOOK NOTES FOR YOU WHILE YOU WERE OUT.

Y-YOU DID THIS FOR ME?! THANK YOU, SHIMOYANAGI-KUN! I'LL TREASURE THIS FOR THE REST OF MY LIFE!
ザワ
MURMUR
TOUCHED
じーん
OH YEAH. I BROUGHT YOU A GIFT, TOO.
APPLE
WHAT?! AN ASTRONAUT'S AUTOGRAPH?!
ザワ
MURMUR
NORI.

OH, HARU-KUN!
...

THIS NORI IS DELICIOUS!
ART
ART

...
スタスタ
スタスタ
SKFF
SKFF
SKFF

ART ROOM
UGH, MITTY!

I THOUGHT YOU WERE GOING TO MAKE UP WITH HARU-KUN!
YOU'RE SUPPOSED TO "SMILE FIRST, AND SMILE LATER!!"
I-I KNOW. I KNOW, BUT!

WHEN I SEE HIS FACE...
I GET WEAK IN THE KNEES.

IT'S OKAY! IF HE DOES HATE YOU, THEN HE MAY NOT MAKE EYE CONTACT WITH YOU ALL THE WAY UNTIL GRAD-UATION.
BUT I!! WILL ALWAYS!! CONSIDER YOUR PROBLEMS MY PROBLEMS!! AND BE READY TO AGONIZE WITH YOU!!
...
DU-DUN

DON'T WORRY, MIZUTANI-SAN.
I'M PRETTY SURE YOSHIDA WANTS TO PATCH THINGS UP, TOO.

IF SASAYAN-KUN SAYS SO, IT MIGHT BE TRUE.
ZOOM
MURMUR
OKAY, THEN! I'LL GO STRAIGHT TO HARU!
MURMUR
ZOOM
OH, YOSHIDA-KUN!
A LITTLE MORE TO THE RIGHT! THE RIGHT!
HURRY! YOU HAVE TO HELP IT!
TREMBLE
IF I GO ANY FARTHER, I'M GONNA FALL, TOO.
TREMBLE

...
PAT
PAT

DAMMIT, SHIZUKU...
SHE MUST BE CRAZY MAD.
SO SHE DOESN'T EVEN WANT TO SEE MY FACE?

WELL, I GUESS I CAN'T BLAME HER.
GO TO HELL.
AFTER WHAT I SAID...
TMP
...I'M PREPARED TO WITHSTAND WHATEVER SHE WANTS TO PUT ME THROUGH.

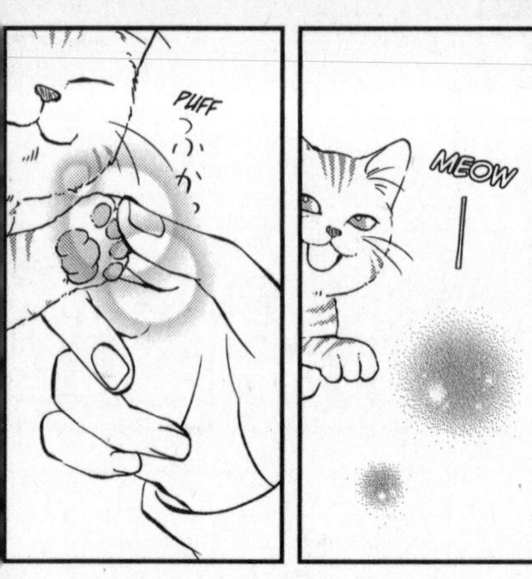
MEOW
PUFF

SO SOOTHING.
PURR PURR PURR
...

I'M USED TO BEING AVOIDED, BUT BEING IGNORED REALLY HURTS.
STILL, IF I DON'T DO SOMETHING, I'LL NEVER BREAK OUT OF THIS.
B-DMP
WHOA, THAT STARTLED ME.
WHAT ARE YOU DOING, YOSHIDA-KUN?

HA HA! COME ON, CUT IT OUT, YOU GUYS!
DON'T FIGHT OVER ME.
BOCK
HISSS

...OKAY.
I'VE BEEN HEALED.
MMK

SHIZUKU.
MURMUR
ザワ
CAN I HAVE A MINUTE?
ザワ
MURMUR
...WE NEED TO TALK.
HE CAME TO ME? THAT MAKE THINGS EASIER.
BAM
...OKAY.

WHAT... WHAT'S GOING ON?
A FIGHT?
MURMUR...
ざわ…
THAT'S UNUSUAL.
MURMUR...
ざわ…
GUTS
じ
...I'M GOING FOR IT!
GUTS
ぐ

...SO.
WHERE DO WE BEGIN?
HUSH
し－ん
...

B-DMP
B-DMP
ドキ
ドキ
I APPRECIATE THAT HARU CAME TO ME.
BUT WHAT IS HE THINKING...?
ちら...
GLANCE

...
I THOUGHT, IF SHE DOESN'T WANT TO SEE MY FACE, I SHOULD COVER IT.
BUT THAT'S JUST MAKING THIS HARDER FOR ME.
PAH...
ぱっ
...

...STILL.
NOW THAT I'M FINALLY SEEING HER FACE AGAIN...

MAYBE I'M IMAGINING IT, BUT...
SHE'S REALLY PRETTY.
I THINK HE JUST HAD SOMETHING OVER HIS HEAD FOR A SECOND?
I WASN'T SURE ABOUT THAT HAIR OF HERS AT FIRST, BUT LOOKING AT IT NOW, IT REALLY FITS.
IT'S EQUALLY DIVIDED ON BOTH SIDES. THAT'S SO SHIZUKU.
I WANT TO RUB MY HAND IN CIRCLES AROUND HER HEAD.
OH, HE'S BACK.
B-DMP B-DMP B-DMP
はっ
GASP!
NO, NO.
THIS ISN'T THE TIME FOR THAT!
SHAKE
SHAKE
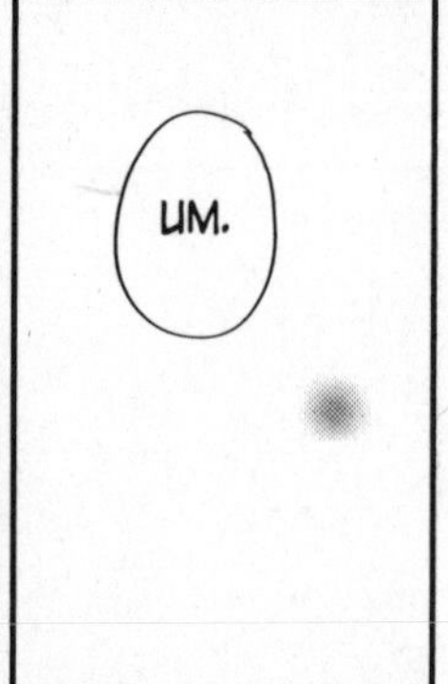
UM.

I'M SORRY, SHIZUKU.

...YEAH.
I WANTED TO APOLOGIZE, TOO.

...

OH.
WHAT A RELIEF.
YOU'RE NOT MAD.

YEAH.
I WAS
AFRAID YOU HATED ME.

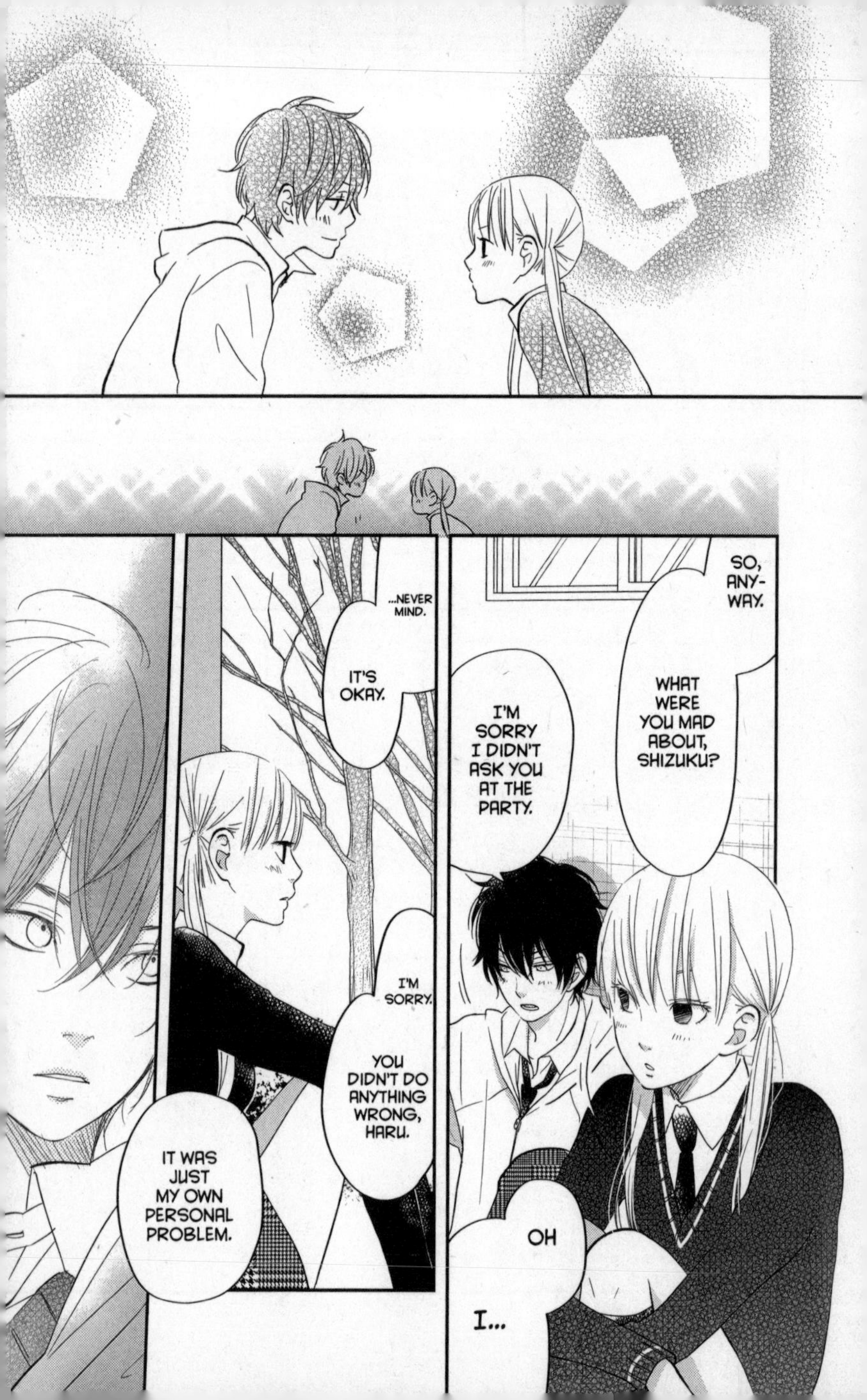
SO, ANYWAY.
WHAT WERE YOU MAD ABOUT, SHIZUKU?
I'M SORRY I DIDN'T ASK YOU AT THE PARTY.
OH
I...
...NEVER MIND.
IT'S OKAY.
I'M SORRY.
YOU DIDN'T DO ANYTHING WRONG, HARU.
IT WAS JUST MY OWN PERSONAL PROBLEM.

EXACTLY.
THAT MEANS
IT'S MY PROBLEM, TOO.

YOU KNOW WHAT I'M LIKE.
I'M SCARED. I'M AFRAID THIS WILL HAPPEN AGAIN.
I DON'T CARE WHAT THE REASON IS. I WANT YOU TO TELL ME.
I WANT TO KNOW HOW YOU FEEL.
ZSH

DING DONG...

...
SHIZUKU?

...

THE BELL RANG!!
?!
THE BELL RANG!!

S-SORRY!
WE HAVE TO GO TO CLASS.

ARE...
ARE YOU A SLAVE TO THE RULES?!
MAYBE THERE WAS SOME-THING WRONG...
...WITH HOW I ASKED?
HOW...
HOW I FEEL?
HOW *DID* I FEEL?
CAN I JUST TELL HIM THAT I WAS JEALOUS BECAUSE WE'RE NOT THE SAME?
IS IT OKAY TO BRING THAT UP AGAIN?
WOULDN'T IT MAKE HIM HATE ME?

HOW DID I USED TO TELL HIM HOW I FELT?
MURMUR
ザワ
MURMUR
ザワ
SHOYO HIGH SCHOOL
MURMUR
ザワ
MURMUR
ザワ
HUH?

WHAT BRINGS YOU HERE, DEAR BROTHER?
DO YOU NEED IYO FOR SOME-THING?
IYO...

SHOYO HIGH
GET LOST.

UNDER-STAND ME? YOU GO STRAIGHT HOME.
DON'T LOOK BACK. JUST GO.
UGH! WHAT'S YOUR PROBLEM?!
YOU'RE ALWAYS SO MEAN TO IYO!
HER BROTHER...?

IS HE FROM KAIMEI ACADEMY?
PSST ヒソ
IS HE WAITING FOR SOMEONE?
PSST ヒソ
STARE
STARE
DAMMIT...STOP STARING AT ME, SHOYO RABBLE.
I'M NOT STANDING HERE BECAUSE I WANT TO.
SHOYO HIGH SCHOOL

UMM... DO YOU HAVE SOME BUSINESS HERE AT OUR SCHOOL?
OH.
SMILE
I'M JUST WAITING FOR SOMEONE.

OH?
YAMAKEN-KUN.

WHAT ARE YOU DOING? THAT UNIFORM STANDS OUT LIKE A SORE THUMB AROUND HERE.
THE POLICE BOX IS RIGHT OVER THERE.
I'M HERE
TO SEE YOU.
SHOYO HIGH

THIS IS THE ONLY WAY
I KNOW I'LL GET IN TOUCH WITH YOU.

SHIZUKU!
YAMAKEN IS TAKING HER AWAY!

BASTARD...
ばっ
BAH

...

BUT IF I GO,
WHAT GOOD WOULD IT DO?

MURMUR
NNN-GH!
MURMUR
WHAT ARE THEY TALKING ABOUT?
I'M SORRY.
I WANNA GO HOME.
UGH! YOU *HAD* TO KEEP DRAGGING YOUR FEET, HARU-KUN! NOW THEY'RE INSIDE!!
HA HA! IT'S LIKE WE'RE PLAYING SPIES!

...WHAT ARE *YOU* DOING HERE, SASAYAN?
HUH? WELL, IT'S NOT TEST SEASON.
SO I'M WORRIED.

DAMMIT, SASAYAN! I WAS ALREADY STARTING TO SUSPECT— YOU'RE JUST HERE FOR LAUGHS, AREN'T YOU?!
YOU GIVE OFF THE SAME SCENT AS YUZAN!
NO, I HALF SINCERELY CARE.
OH! THEY CAME OUT-SIDE!!

SO I THOUGHT I WOULD GO AHEAD AND PERFECT MY VOCABULARY FIRST.
NO, IT WOULD BE MORE EFFICIENT TO DO SOME OLD PROBLEMS, AND LOOK UP ANY WORDS YOU DON'T KNOW AS YOU GO ALONG.
MURMUR
MURMUR
WELL.

IT'S GREAT THAT I GOT HER OUT HERE, BUT AS USUAL, HER TOPICS OF CONVERSATION ARE LIMITED BEYOND ALL REASON.
COME TO THINK OF IT, KOBUNSHA JUST RELEASED A GUIDEBOOK, BUT THE QUESTIONS STARTED LOOKING A LOT LIKE THE ONES FROM AN '05 BOOK FROM A DIFFERENT PUBLISHER, SO I LOOKED, AND SURE ENOUGH, IT WAS COMPILED BY ODA-SAN.
FRAPPUCCINO...
AND THE CONTENT IS GETTING MORE AND MORE OBSCURE. I CAN'T QUITE FOLLOW THIS.

AND...
BUT-WHATEVER. NOW IS NOT THE TIME TO LET THAT BOTHER ME.
...I CAN SEE SOMETHING OVER THERE LOOKING SHIFTILY AT ME.
I MADE IT THIS FAR.
APPUCCINO...!!
SSIP...

SO
HOW ARE THINGS WITH HARU?

...

PFFFT
ズボ

I...
I THINK WE'VE MADE UP.
PROBABLY.

LOOK.
I'M FAIRLY CERTAIN
I'M A BETTER MATCH FOR YOU.

DO YOU WANT TO KEEP REPEATING WHATEVER IT IS YOU'RE DOING FOR ALL TIME?
WHAT YOU TWO HAVE ISN'T A ROMANTIC RELATIONSHIP.

I'M HERE TO ASK YOU ONE MORE TIME.
WILL YOU BE MY GIRLFRIEND?

NNNN-
NGH!
I CAN'T MAKE OUT A THING THEY'RE SAYING!

UGH, HARU-KUN! WHY ARE YOU SO QUIET?! SHOULDN'T YOU GO STOP THEM?!
...

MURMUR
ザワ
MURMUR
ザワー
MURMUR
ザワ

FIELD OF VISION

I BOUGHT SOME ODEN!
PATTER PATTER
たたた
LOST AT ROCK-PAPER-SCISSORS

SERI-OUSLY.
NERVES NERVES
ハラハラ
WAAAH
DON'T GO BUYING ODEN WHEN YOU'RE TAILING SOMEONE.
TOO DISTRACTED BY THEIR INCOMPETENCE TO CONCEN-TRATE.
SO THE COMPILER, ODA-SAN...

BRRRR

...IS IT GETTING COLD OUT HERE?
ALL OF A SUDDEN.
ガタガタ
BRR BRR
SERIOUSLY.
WHY WOULD YOU ORDER THAT IN THE MIDDLE OF WINTER?

FRAPPUCCINO

EVER SINCE YUZAN-SAN TREATED HER TO ONE IN VOLUME 10, CHAPTER 37, SHE'S BEEN WANTING TO TRY ONE AGAIN.

IT WAS EXPENSIVE, BUT SHE INDULGED AND GOT THE TALL.

"I'M HERE TO ASK YOU ONE MORE TIME."
"WILL YOU BE MY GIRL-FRIEND?"
...WHAT'S WITH THE FACE?
I...I'M SORRY. I JUST DIDN'T SEE THAT COMING.
I THOUGHT WE WERE DONE WITH ALL OF THAT!
WELL SORRY FOR DIGGING UP THE PAST.

THE REASON I CAN'T BE FRIENDS WITH YOU...
IS THAT I STILL HAVE THESE FEELINGS FOR YOU.

"DID YOU GET SCARED"
"THAT YOU'D GET HURT?"
YES, I'M SCARED.
I THOUGHT I WOULD NEVER STOOP SO LOW AS TO KEEP PURSUING A GIRL AFTER SHE REJECTED ME.
BUT THEN I SEE HER, AND THIS IS WHAT HAPPENS.

WE MAY HAVE HIT A ROUGH PATCH, BUT I AM TECHNICALLY HARU'S GIRLFRIEND.
DON'T YOUR MORALS SAY ANYTHING ABOUT THAT, YAMAKEN-KUN?
BEING FACED WITH THE REAL THING JUST PACKS A HARDER PUNCH.
THAT WAS THE LAST QUESTION I WANTED HER TO ASK ME.

...I JUST TOLD YOU, DIDN'T I?
I'M A BETTER MATCH OR YOU, IZUTANI-SAN.

I WOULDN'T MAKE YOU SO NERVOUS.
I WOULDN'T MAKE YOU WORRY.
I WOULD
TAKE BETTER CARE OF YOU.
ザワザワ
MURMUR MURMUR
NNN-NGH!
I SENSE UNREST BETWEEN THEM...

COME ON, HARU-KUN!! WHY AREN'T YOU STOPPING THIS?! YOU'RE HER BOYFRIEND, AREN'T YOU?!
RAR
W-WELL, THEY MIGHT JUST BE ARGUING ABOUT THE CURRENT STATE OF TEACHING MATERIALS.
HOW CAN YOU SAY THAT?! ARE YOU EVEN AWAKE?!
ARRRGH! WE'RE MARCHING FORWARD, MEN!!
SHOONK
...HEY, SASAYAN. WHAT EXACTLY DO YOU SEE IN HER?
...NO COMMENT.
ANYWAY, YOSHIDA. HAVE YOU TALKED TO MIZUTANI-SAN?
YOU PATCHED THINGS UP WITH HER, RIGHT?
RUSTLE
WE SHOULD CATCH HER BEFORE SHE GETS SPOTTED.
RUSTLE
...I THINK SO.
BUT I DON'T KNOW IF WE DISCUSSED THE PROBLEM.
SO LET'S PULL NATSUME OUT OF THE BUSHES AND GET OUT OF HERE, SASAYAN.
I'M AFRAID OF WHAT I MIGHT END UP DOING!!
I FEEL LIKE I COULD POUNCE ON THEM AT ANY MOMENT.
OH, SO YOU *WERE* HOLDING BACK.
SHUDDER SHUDDER
YOU SAID YOU WANTED
TO BE FRIENDS.
RUSTLE RUSTLE
!!

THAT MEANS THAT YOU NEED ME, AT LEAST A LITTLE, DOESN'T IT?
IF YOU GO OUT WITH ME, WE CAN ENCOURAGE EACH OTHER IN OUR STUDIES THROUGH FRIENDLY COMP-ETITION.
I'LL JUST HAVE TO ATTACK HER WITH LOGIC.

F...FRIENDLY COMP-ETITION...?
THAT'S RIGHT.
AS WE FACE COLLEGE ENTRANCE EXAMS.
THOUGH I'D HATE NOTHING MORE.

OH! SHE'S TAKING THE BAIT.
THAT LITTLE...
BRUSH HIM OFF!
BRUSH HIM OFF, SHIZUKU!

...

YOU...YOU'RE ACTUALLY CONSIDERING IT?!
...!

S-SO WHAT'S SO GREAT ABOUT THAT?!
?!
ZSH
HARU-KUN HAS A LOT OF GOOD POINTS, TOO, YOU KNOW!
HARU-KUN L—
LIKES ANIMALS AND STUFF!!
...
PSH!!

EEP!
SLUMP!!
SHOONK
カックン!!
ズボッ
...
SIGH...
N... NATSUME-SAN?!
ARE YOU TAKING THE NEXT TRIAL EXAM?
CLATTER
ガタ
HUH?
UH, YES.
THEN I'LL TALK TO YOU THEN.
IF IT'S ALL RIGHT,
KEEP THAT AFTER-NOON FREE.
MURMUR
ザワ
...
MURMUR
ザワ

ZSH...
SO...
WHAT ARE YOU DOING?
ALL OF YOU.
GULP

WE—
WE WERE ON OUR WAY TO GET SOME TAIYAKI.

I'M SORRY, I'M SORRY, I'M SORRY.
IDIOT.

I'M
KIND OF TIRED.
"I WOULD
"TAKE BETTER CARE OF YOU."
EXACTLY. THAT MEANS
IT'S MY PROBLEM, TOO.
WHY
COULDN'T I ANSWER HIM?

HE MADE ME SO HAPPY.
I WANT TO KNOW HOW YOU FEEL.
BUT
WHAT WOULD I HAVE SAID?
I WAS JEALOUS OF HARU, AND FRUSTRATED AT MYSELF.
AND PART OF ME STILL FEELS THAT WAY.
THAT DAY...
OH, I GET IT.

...I HURT HARU....
...TO AVOID GETTING HURT MYSELF.
WHAT AM I FREAKING OUT ABOUT?
THAT'S NOT WHAT I WANTED TO TALK TO HER ABOUT ANYWAY.
...DAMMI
I COULDN ACTUALLY TALK TO HER ABOU IT.

HEY...
...YAMAKEN-KUN?
YOU STARTLED ME.
...UH.
OH.
I THOUGHT YOU WERE CRYING.
...

OF COURSE.
THIS IS WHAT I SHOULD HAVE SAID.

I LOVE YOU.

CHAPTER 44: YAMAKEN AND SHIZUKU

SHOONG SHOONG SHOONG SHOONG
SHIZUK HAS ALWA BEEN
FAIRLY LOW MAINTENANCE.
SHE'S JUST A KID, BUT SOMETIMES SHE'S MORE RATIONAL THAN I AM.
SHE EVEN COOKS HER OWN SEKIHAN.
AND THAT'S WHY I WORRY ABOUT HER.
...OH, BUT
THERE WAS ONE TIME.

THAT FIRS YEAR YOSHI SAN WENT WORK.
AFTER SHIZUKU SAW HER OFF, JUST ONCE
SHE MADE THIS REALLY ODD FACE.
LIKE SHE WAS ANGRY, BUT LIKE SHE WAS CRYING.
OR LIKE SHE WAS EATING A REALLY SOUR UMEBOSHI.
WHEN I SAW IT, MY FIRST THOUGHT WAS THAT I DIDN'T EVER WANT TO SEE THAT LOOK ON HER FACE AGAIN.
BUT LOOKING BACK ON IT NOW,
I WISH I'D LET HER MAKE THAT FACE MORE OFTEN.

...
UH, UM.
YAMA-KEN-KUN.
...
SORRY.
I THOUGHT YOU WERE CRYING.
AND I JUST...
UH, NO.
I WAS COLD.

...
HRRNK
ちーん
CAN I...
STAY HERE A WHILE?
JUST UNTIL THE BUS GETS HERE.
...

WH...
WHY ISN'T HE SAYING ANYTHING?
...

OH, THERE'S THE BUS.
VROOM...
ブロロ...
...UM, YAMAKEN-KUN.
BYE...

...HEY.
THINK ABOUT IT.
JUST ONCE. REALLY THINK ABOUT IT, OKAY?

OKAY.

...OR SO I SAID.
チュン チュン
CHIRP CHIRP
I OULDN'T SLEEP A WINK...
BUT HOW EXACTLY
AM I SUPPOSED TO "REALLY THINK" ABOUT IT?
ボー…
DAAAZE...
しゃこしゃこ
BRUSH BRUSH BRUSH
LIKE, DO A COMPARISON STUDY?
"I LOVE YOU."

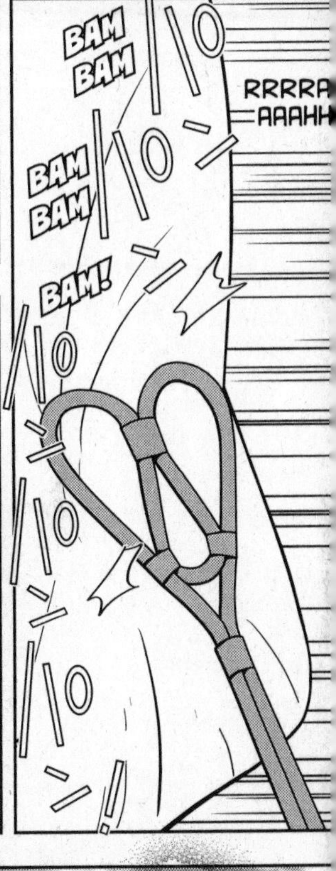
RRRRA
AAAHH
BAM
BAM
BAM
BAM
BAM!

YOU'RE WORKING AWFULLY HARD, SIS...
TAK-AYA.
HAVE FUN AT SOCCER.
HUFF HUFF
I...LIKE IT WHEN GIRLS WEAR THEIR HAIR DOWN.

...IT'S A BEAUTIFUL DAY.

MURMUR
ザワ
MURMUR
ザワ

EDIT
MESSAGES
Are you free today? Let's get together!
I'm busy.

I SAID IT!! I CAN'T BELIEVE I SAID IT!!
...IF YOU'RE GONNA STARE AT ME, YOU COULD SAY SOMETHING.
OH.
I DIDN'T WANT TO INTERRUPT.

I SAW YOU FROM ABOUT 50 METERS OFF, BUT YOU WOULD SMILE TO YOURSELF, AND THEN WRITHE IN AGONY. YOU LOOKED LIKE YOU WERE HAVING SO MUCH FUN, I DIDN'T WANT TO BOTHER YOU.
HEY, STOP IT. DON'T SAY THAT.
YOU'RE GETTING MORE AND MORE LIKE YOUR DAMN BROTHER.

LATER.

...HARU.

I...
...TOLD MIZUTANI-SAN HOW I FEEL ABOUT HER.

OH.
...

CALL FROM SHIZUKU MIZUTANI
SWER
IGNORE
PUBLIC LIBRARY
OH, HELLO, YAMAKEN-KUN? THIS IS MIZUTANI.
WILL YOU COME SEE ME?

OH, YAMAKEN-KUN.
...HELLO.

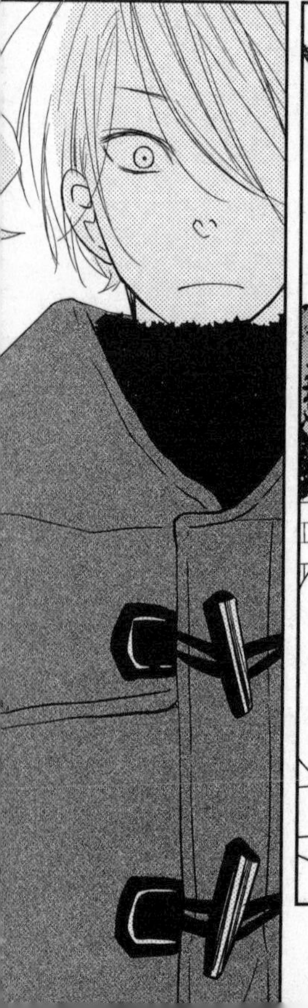

...
WHAT'S WITH THE HAIR?
OH, THIS?
MY BROTHER SAID HE LIKES IT BETTER THIS WAY.
ANYWAY, YAMAKEN-KUN, YOU'RE AN HOUR LATE.

...
I...
COULDN'T SLEEP LAST NIGHT.
EVEN AFTER I GOT HOME, I COULDN'T GET YOU OUT OF MY HEAD.
I DIDN'T SEE MUCH POINT IN BROODING, SO I FIGURED I MIGHT AS WELL TRY STUDYING AT THE LIBRARY.
BUT I COULDN'T CONCEN-TRATE.

...YAMAKEN-KUN.
WHAT DO YOU SEE IN ME?
WH... WHAT?
IS THIS AN INTERVIEW?

...I LIKE THAT YOU'RE SO GENUINE.
YOU'RE STRAIGHT-FORWARD,
AND HONEST TO A FAULT.
UNLIKE ME,
YOU CAN ACTUALLY TELL PEOPLE WHAT YOU'RE FEELING.

SO ARE YOU ALWAYS THINKING THINGS YOU CAN'T SAY OUT LOUD, YAMAKEN-KUN?
...IT'S REALLY HARD
NOT TO EMBELLISH.

ESPECIALLY WHEN I'M TALKING TO THE GIRL I LIKE.
I THINK...
YOU'RE ALWAYS HELPING ME OUT.
WHEN I'M WITH YOU,
I CAN STAY CALM AND COLLECTED.
I CAN BE MY USUAL SELF.
AND THAT WAS VERY COMFORTABLE.

...ON THE OTHER HAND, WHEN I'M WITH HARU, HE EXHAUSTS ME TO THE CORE OF MY BEING.
TCH.
チッ
HE MAKES ME ANGRY, HE SURPRISES ME.
HE HAS THE AUDACITY TO SURPASS MY EXPECTATIONS EVERY SINGLE DAY.
...HE MAKES ME WONDER.
DID I ALWAYS...
...HAVE ALL THESE EMOTIONS?
MAYBE YOU'RE RIGHT, YAMAKEN-KUN.
MAYBE WHAT WE HAVE CAN'T BE CALLED A ROMANTIC RELATIONSHIP.
BUT I'M OKAY WITH THAT.
I LIKE IT.

SO I'M SORRY, YAMAKEN-KUN.
I CAN'T BE YOUR GIRLFRIEND.
!

...UH, UM, YAMAKEN-KUN.
WERE YOU LISTENING TO ME?
I WAS LISTENING.
AT LEAST
LET ME DREAM ONE LAST TIME.
I KNEW...
I KNEW YOU'D ONLY MAKE THAT FACE...
...
...IN FRONT OF HARU.
WELL.
DON'T REGRET YOUR CHOICE.
PAH
はっ
YOU'LL NEVER MEET...
...ANOTHER GUY AS GOOD AS ME.

THANK YOU.
YAMAKEN-KUN.
...I KNOW.
IDIOT.
THAT'S BACK-WARDS.
I DOUBT I'LL EVER MEET...
...ANOTHER GIRL AS GOOD AS YOU.
HEY.
YOU SAID YOU WANTED TO BE FRIENDS, RIGHT?

WELL.
YOU'RE ABOUT THE ONLY WOMAN WHO COULD EVER DATE THAT MORON HARU.
I THINK IT'LL GET PRETTY TOUGH.
SO I GUESS I COULD
DO YOU THE FAVOR OF BEING YOUR FRIEND.
...I FINALLY FIGURED IT OUT.
YOU'RE REALLY NOT GENUINE AT ALL, ARE YOU?
SHUT UP.

...I'D LOVE THAT.

I WANT
TO SEE HARU.
AND THE FIRST THING I'LL DO
IS APOLOGIZE.
TELL HIM I WANT TO RECONCILE.
AND EXPLAIN TO HIM HOW I FEEL.
OKAY.
NOW THAT'S SETTLED, IT'S TIME TO CALL HIM.
KA-POP

WHAT DOES THIS MARK MEAN?
I NEVER NOTICED IT BEFORE.
BUT IT COMES UP SOME-TIMES.
RUMMAGE RUMMAGE
WHERE WAS THAT MANUAL?
VOICE MAIL.
USER'S GUIDE
WHAT? THIS DATE.
THAT'S THE DAY OF YUZAN-SAN'S PARTY...
...HELLO?
IS THIS SHIZUKU?
ズダーン
SLAM!
THAT HURT, DAMMIT! I TOLD YOU TO NOT TO DRIVE LIKE A MANIAC!!
WHAT IS HE DOING? SERIOUSLY.
...UM.
SOMETHING'S COME UP, SO I'M GONNA BE AWAY FOR ABOUT TWO WEEKS.
I DIDN'T WANT YOU TO WORRY, SO I CALLED TO LET YOU KNOW.

"NEXT TIME YOU GO ANYWHERE, I WANT YOU CALL TH NUMBER, OKAY?
"OKAY. I GOT IT."
HE ACTUALLY ...
...KEPT HIS PROMISE.
I THINK I'LL...
...HAVE COOLED DOWN BY THE TIME I GET BACK.
SO
LET'S TALK IT OVER AGAIN.
WAS HE THINKING ABOUT ME
ALL THIS TIME?
MISA BATT CENT
PLAY THE NEWEST ARCADE GAMES!
MISAKI BATTING CENTER NOW ACCEPTING MEMBER-SHIPS!

HARU.

...SHI-ZUKU.

I HEARD YOUR VOICE MAIL.
WHAT *WAS* THAT ABOUT?
...*YOU'RE* THE ONE WHO TOLD ME TO CALL IF I WENT SOME-WHERE.
I'M NOT GONNA EXPECT YOU
TO CALL ME UNDER THOSE CIRCUM-STANCES.

...OH REALLY.
WELL EXCUSE ME FOR BEING CLUELESS.
A—
ANYWAY, HARU.
YOU'RE ALWAYS SO IMPETUOUS.
LIKE THAT DAY.
I...
I WAS ALREADY FREAKING OUT BECAUSE I'M SUDDENLY AT THIS FANCY PARTY.
AND THEN YOU GO OFF BY YOURSELF,
YOU LEAVE ME ALL ALONE...
...AND?

IT...IT MAKES ME ANGRY THAT I WORK HARDER THAN YOU BUT YOU'RE A BETTER STUDENT.
IT MAKES ME ANGRY THAT UNLIKE ME,
YOU DON'T HAVE TO DO ANYTHING TO GET PEOPLE TO CARE ABOUT YOU.
IT MAKES ME ANGRY THAT I END UP FEELING BAD
FOR THINKING THESE TERRIBLE THINGS.
STUPID HARU.
IT'S ALL YOUR FAULT.

SIGH...
はあっ…
...

WHAT ELSE?

YOU...
REALLY LET PEOPLE HAVE IT, DON'T YOU, SHIZUKU?

ポロポロポロ…
DRIP DRIP DRIP...
WH—
WHAT HAPPENED?!
DOES YOUR STOMACH HURT OR SOME-THING?
...NO.

CONTINUED IN VOLUME 12!!

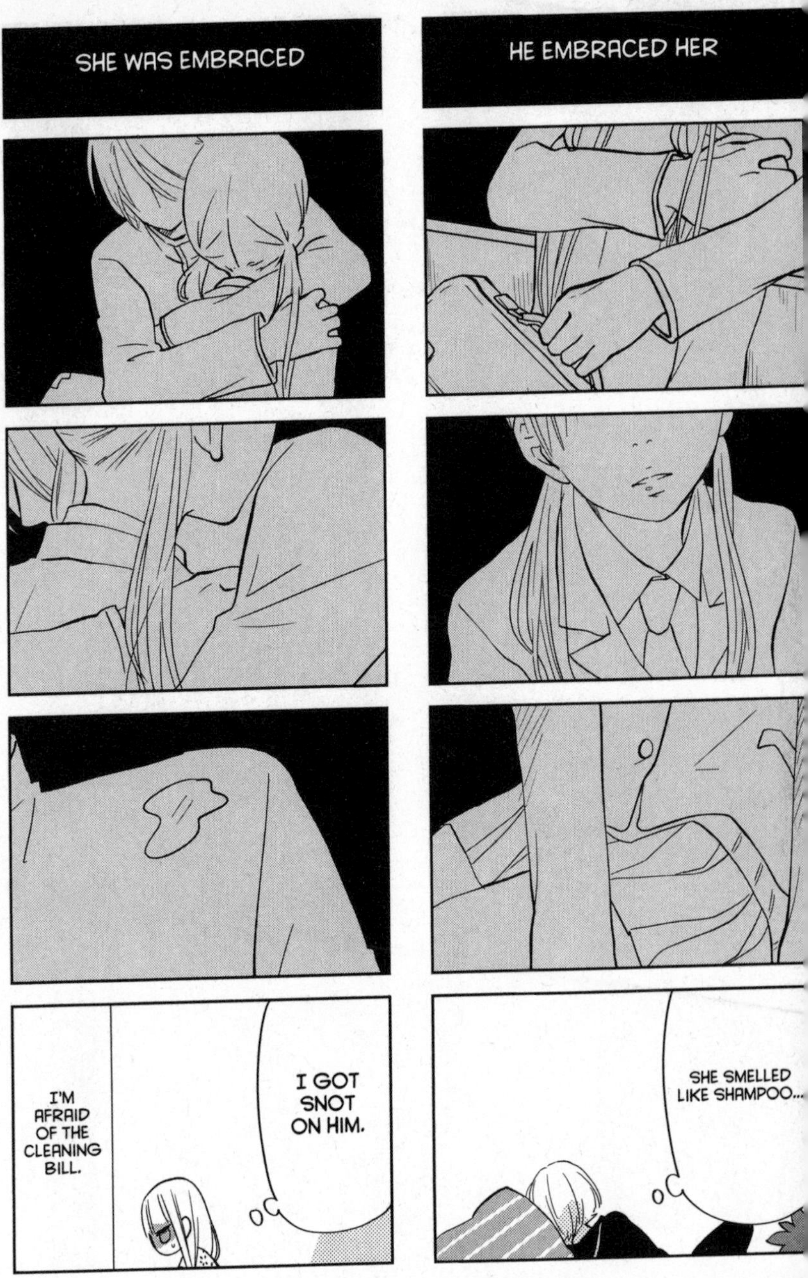

HE EMBRACED HER

SHE SMELLED LIKE SHAMPOO...

SHE WAS EMBRACED

I GOT SNOT ON HIM.

I'M AFRAID OF THE CLEANING BILL.

BONUS MANGA 1

BACK IN FIRST YEAR

I HAVE A LOT OF FRIENDS.
I LIKE SCHOOL.
I HATE TESTS.
WHAT DO I THINK ABOUT?
NORMAL STUFF.

OH, IT'S NATSUME-SAN.
REMEMBER THIS IS BACK IN FIRST YEAR.

SIGH, SHE'S SO PRETTY.
AND I GET TO BE IN HER CLASS. I'M A HAPPY MAN.
I'M SO GLAD I CAME TO THIS SCHOOL
YEAH. SHE IS PRETTY.
I HEAR SHE'S ALREADY REJECTED OUR WHOLE ROSTER OF REGULARS.
SO IT'S TRUE SHE HATES MEN.

BUT I PREFER MORE UPBEAT GIRLS.
OH, IT'S YOSHIDA-KUN.
WHAT'S THE NAME OF THAT GIRL THAT'S ALWAYS WITH HIM?
MIZUTANI-SAN, RIGHT?
MELON BUN

ROLL...

HEY, YOU DROPPED YOUR ERASER.
...

...HUH? WHAT?!
SHE IGNORED ME?
WHY?
AND WHAT DO I DO WITH THIS?

WHAT A JERK.
AND YET...

...FATE MADE US FRIENDS.
HOME CENTER
...SO DO YOU THINK YOU COULD PICK UP THE STUFF, NATSUME-SAN?
THOSE GUYS COULD STILL BE AROUND.
I'LL HELP YOU CARRY IT.

...

...
I DON'T THINK I CAN GET ALONG WITH HER.
SHE ALMOST ONLY EVER SMILES AT YOSHIDA AND MIZUTANI-SAN.
IT'S POSSIBLE THAT I ONLY FEEL LIKE WE'RE FRIENDS BECAUSE THEY'RE AROUND.
I CAN'T REALLY TELL WHAT SHE'S THINKING.
...SO... UM.

THE TRUTH IS,
SINCE I'VE MADE FRIENDS WITH MITTY AND HARU-KUN,
EVERY DAY, I'M SURPRISED AT HOW HAPPY MY LIFE IS.
?
OKAY.

SO, SINCE YOU'RE PART OF THE GROUP...
...IF *THEY* LIKE YOU, THEN I THINK I WOULD LIKE TO HAVE A PEACEFUL, FRIENDLY RELATIONSHIP WITH YOU, TOO.

OH.
OKAY.
THEN LET'S BE FRIENDS, NATSUME-SAN.

...ARE YOU SURE?
WOW.
YEAH.
SHE'S ACTUALLY PRETTY NICE.
...OH, GOOD!
ACTUALLY, I WAS SO WORRIED THAT YOU WOULD GET A CRUSH ON ME.

IT HAPPENS, YOU KNOW. A GUY WILL PRETEND TO BE MY FRIEND, AND THEN HIT ME WITH A SURPRISE ATTACK.
OH, BUT DON'T DO THAT, OKAY, SASAYAN-KUN?
...OKAY.
I DON'T THINK THAT'LL BE A PROBLEM.
I SAID.
BUT I'M GONNA END UP FALLING IN LOVE WITH HER SOONER OR LATER (PROBABLY).
THAT'S A STORY FOR ANOTHER TIME.

★ BONUS MANGA 1 ★ END

WHAT?!
WHAT'S THE MATTER, NATSUME-SAN?
IT... IT'S YU-CHAN...
TOBITA-KUN CAME TO VISIT OVER THE LONG HOLIDAY...
...AND SHE BECAME A *WOMAN.*

END OF VOLUME BONUS MANGA 2 "GIRLS' STUDY GROUP"

?
NO BOYS ALLOWED

WHAT? YOU WANT ME TO TELL YOU ABOUT MY EXPERI-ENCE?
OH, COME ON, GIRLS.
YOU'RE MAKING ME BLUSH.

PLEASE TELL US!
HEALTH AND PHYSICAL EDUCATION

IT WAS MY FIRST TIME, TOO. I DON'T THINK I HAVE A LOT TO TELL.
BUT I CAN GIVE YOU A FEW IM-PRESSIONS.

FIRST, IT HURTS.
AND IT'S KINDA GROSS.
I NEVER WANT TO DO IT AGAIN.

IT...IT'S THAT BAD?
IT'S LIKE YOU'RE BEING SQUEEZED BY A VICE.

WORKING UP TO IT, TOKITA-KUN AND I BOTH GOT PRETTY FREAKED OUT, SO WE WENT FOR IT, AND THEN IT WAS OVER.
IT WAS AFTER THAT THAT THE PAIN STARTED CREEPING UP ON ME.
JUST... JUST WENT FOR IT?
WENT FOR WHAT?!
HOW?!

BUT MORE THAN ANY-THING,
THE FEAR WHEN IT STARTS TO COME IN...
AAAA-AAHH
C-COME IN...!!
YU-CHAN, YOU'RE SO BOLD!
THAT'S AN ALL-GIRLS' SCHOOL STUDENT FOR YOU!

I WAS SO, SO SCARED.
I CRIED A LITTLE.
BUT TOKITA-KUN HELD MY HAND THE WHOLE TIME.
AND WHEN I LOOKED AT HIS FACE,
I THOUGHT, I CAN DO ANYTHING WITH HIM.
AND THEN I DIDN'T MIND THE PAIN SO MUCH.

YU-CHAN...!!
CLAP CLAP CLAP...
HA HA. I CAN'T BELIEVE I TOLD YOU ABOUT IT.
WELL, AS ONE WITH EXPERIENCE, THERE'S ONLY ONE THING I CAN SAY.

THE SOONER YOU GET YOUR WISDOM TEETH PULLED, THE BETTER.
I THINK THAT ABOUT SUMS IT UP.

TELLLL...
YO-SAN, WILL YOU ANSWER THE PHONE?
CONTINUED IN VOLUME 12
BONUS
IYO LEARNED A LOT...FROM WHAT YOU TOLD US.
OH! SO YOU'RE...

★BONUS MANGA 2★ END

COMMENT

Robico

In my comment for volume one,
I said I felt that the characters
are totally unrelated to me, but
now I'm starting to finally feel like
they're my neighbors. It's already
volume 11. I feel like it's taken a
long time, and no time at all.

KA-CLANK
KA-CLUNK
KA-CLANK
KA-CLUNK
MY NAME IS MITTY DU AMORE SHIZUKU.
STARTING TODAY,
CREEEEEEAK
WELCOME.
TO YOSHIDA ACADEMY.
I WILL BE ATTENDING THE ROYAL MAGIC ACADEMY
ON A SPECIAL SCHOLAR-SHIP.
ZOO-ZOOM...

DURING THE SCHOOL YEAR, I BECAME FRIENDS WITH A MASTER OF THE SUPER POWERFUL MAGIC VALUSE, AND A MASTER OF INTER-DIMENSIONAL MAGIC.
THERE'S NO TELLING... WHEN I MIGHT LOSE CONTROL.
SO EVERYONE CALLS ME THE POP-UP PIRATE.
MY GOAL
SIZZLE
SIZZ SIZZ SIZZLE
WHERE AM I?
BUT NEVER MIND THAT.
OPEN SESAME!
FLASH
IS TO MASTER THIS MAGICAL CUISINE AND USE IT TO REBUILD MY FAMILY RESTAURANT.
PATTER PATTER PATTER...
OH, SASAYAN-KUN! TURNING INTO A BLACK CAT AGAIN!
MEOW
MEW MEW
NATSUME-SAN, DON'T BRING YOUR WITCH'S BROOM INTO THE COOKING ROOM.
...EXCUSE ME.
MAY I ASK WHO MADE
THE LOVE POTION FRIED RICE?
THE CURTAIN OPENS ON ANOTHER COOKING SHOW-DOWN.
VILLAIN AGAIN

Translation notes

Japanese is a tricky language for most Westerners, and translation is often more art than science. For your edification and reading pleasure, here are notes on some of the places where we could have gone in a different direction in our translation of the work, or where a Japanese cultural reference is used.

The commercial high school's Four Heavenly Kings, page 8

A commercial high school, or shogyo koko, is a high school that focuses on teaching kids about business, economics, and other subjects related to commerce—training them to go into business right after high school rather than preparing them for college. The "Four Heavenly Kings" is taken from a Buddhist belief in four gods that rule over the four cardinal directions. The name has come to be used in manga, anime, and video games to refer to groups of four people who are unbeatable in their given field (usually fighting).

Slave to the rules, page 102

Here Haru actually accused Shizuku of having a government job, using the term "*yakusho shigoto*." This particular word for "government job" is often used in a derogatory manner, to describe someone or something that places a stronger emphasis on following the rules than on maintaining interpersonal relationships. In other words, Shizuku cares more about being in class on time than about continuing this very important conversation.

Police box, page 105

Shizuku suggests that Yamaken is looking for a "*koban*," which is like a miniature police station. They are spread throughout the community, bringing the police close to the community so they can respond more readily to the citizens' needs. A common need that is met by police at these police boxes is to give directions to people who are lost.

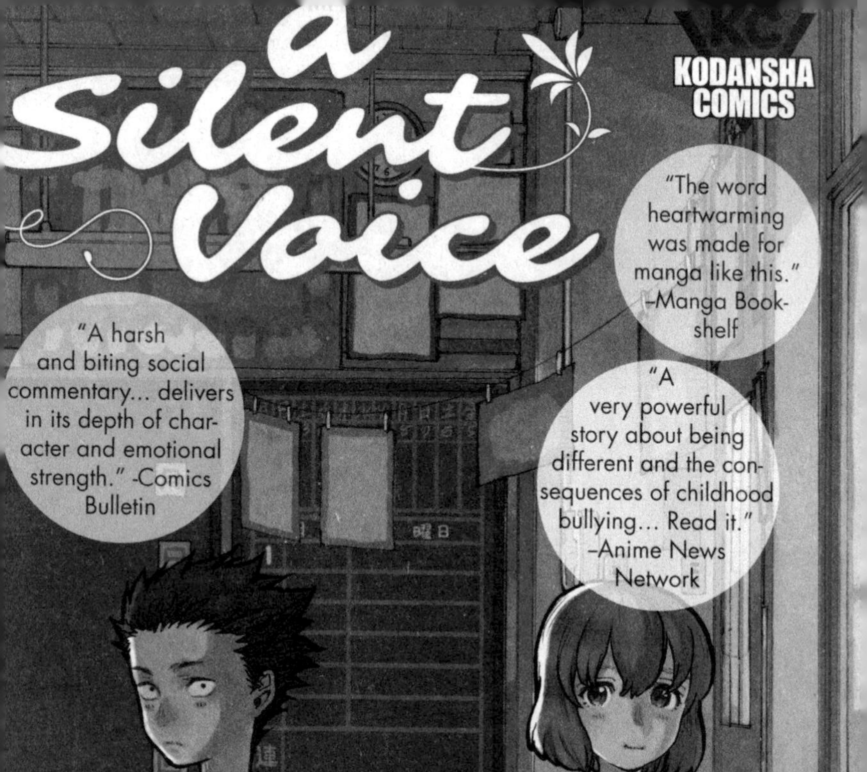

a Silent Voice
KODANSHA COMICS
"The word heartwarming was made for manga like this." –Manga Bookshelf
"A harsh and biting social commentary... delivers in its depth of character and emotional strength." -Comics Bulletin
"A very powerful story about being different and the consequences of childhood bullying... Read it." –Anime News Network

"The show provides a pleasant window on the highs and lows of young love with two young people who are first timers at the real thing."
-The Fandom Post
"Always it is smarter, more poetic, more touching, just plain better than you think it is going to be."
-Anime News Network
Say I Love You.
KC
KODANSHA COMICS

My Little Monster volume 11 is a work of fiction. Names, characters, places, and incidents are the products of the author's imagination or are used fictitiously. Any resemblance to actual events, locales, or persons, living or dead, is entirely coincidental.

A Kodansha Comics Trade Paperback Original.

Published in the United States by Kodansha Comics, an imprint of Kodansha USA Publishing, LLC, New York.

Publication rights for this English edition arranged through Kodansha Ltd., Tokyo.

First published in Japan in 2013 by Kodansha Ltd., Tokyo as *Tonari no Kaibutsu-kun*, volume 11.

ISBN 978-1-63236-108-0

Printed in the United States of America.

www.kodanshacomics.com

9 8 7 6 5 4 3 2 1

Translator: Alethea Nibley & Athena Nibley
Lettering: Paige Pumphrey